Starter: 150 vocabulary words

Ten Brothers

十兄弟

叶婵娟 改编

Download Online
www.sinolingua.com.cn

First Edition   2016

ISBN 978-7-5138-1064-7
Copyright 2016 by Sinolingua Co., Ltd
Published by Sinolingua Co., Ltd
24 Baiwanzhuang Road, Beijing 100037, China
Tel: (86) 10-68320585 68997826
Fax: (86) 10-68997826 68326333
http://www.sinolingua.com.cn
E-mail: hyjx@sinolingua.com.cn
Facebook: www.facebook.com/sinolingua
Printed by Beijing Jinghua Hucais Printing Co., Ltd

Printed in the People's Republic of China

编者的话

对于广大汉语学习者来说,要想快速提高汉语水平,扩大阅读量是很有必要的。"彩虹桥"汉语分级读物为汉语学习者提供了一系列有趣、有用的汉语阅读材料。本系列读物按照词汇量进行分级,并通过精彩的故事叙述,给读者带来了丰富有趣的阅读享受。本套读物主要有以下特点:

一、分级精准,循序渐进。我们参考了新汉语水平考试(HSK)词汇表(2012年修订版)、《汉语国际教育用音节汉字词汇等级划分(国家标准)》和《常用汉语1500高频词语表》等词汇分级标准,结合《欧洲语言教学与评估框架性共同标准》(CEFR),设计了一套适合汉语学习者的"彩虹桥"词汇分级标准。本系列读物分为7个级别(入门级*、1级、2级、3级、4级、5级、6级),供不同水平的汉语学习者选择,每个级别故事的生词数量不超过本级别对应词汇量的20%。随着级别的升高,故事的篇幅逐渐加长。本系列读物与HSK、CEFR的对应级别,各级词汇量以及每本书的字数详见下表。

---

* 入门级(Starter)在封底用S标识。

级别	入门级	1级	2级	3级	4级	5级	6级
对应级别	HSK1 CEFR A1	HSK1-2 CEFR A1-A2	HSK2-3 CEFR A2-B1	HSK3 CEFR A2-B1	HSK3-4 CEFR B1	HSK4 CEFR B1-B2	HSK5 CEFR B2-C1
词汇量	150	300	500	750	1 000	1 500	2 500
字数	1 000	2 500	5 000	7 500	10 000	15 000	25 000

二、**故事精彩，题材多样**。本套读物选材的标准就是"精彩"，所选的故事要么曲折离奇，要么感人至深，对读者构成奇妙的吸引力。选题广泛取材于中国的神话传说、民间故事、文学名著、名人传记和历史故事等，让汉语学习者在阅读中潜移默化地了解中国的文化和历史。

三、**结构合理，实用性强**。"彩虹桥"系列读物的每一本书中，除了中文故事正文之外，都配有主要人物的中英文介绍、生词英文注释及例句、故事正文的英文翻译、练习题以及生词表，方便读者阅读和理解故事内容，提升汉语阅读能力。练习题主要采用客观题，题型多样，难度适中，并附有参考答案，既可供汉语教师在课堂上教学使用，又可供汉语学习者进行自我水平检测。

如果您对本系列读物有什么想法，比如推荐精彩故事、提出改进意见等，请发邮件到 liuxiaolin@sinolingua.com.cn，与我们交流探讨。也可以关注我们的微信公众号 CHQRainbowBridge，随时与我们交流互动。同时，微信公众号会不定期发布有关"彩虹桥"的出版信息，以及汉语阅读、中国文化小知识等。

韩 颖　刘小琳

Preface

For students who study Chinese as a foreign language, it's crucial for them to enlarge the scope of their reading to improve their comprehension skills. The "Rainbow Bridge" Graded Chinese Reader series is designed to provide a collection of interesting and useful Chinese reading materials. This series grades each volume by its vocabulary level and brings the learners into every scene through vivid storytelling. The series has the following features:

I. A gradual approach by grading the volumes based on vocabulary levels. We have consulted the New HSK Vocabulary (2012 Revised Edition), the *Graded Chinese Syllables, Characters and Words for the Application of Teaching Chinese to the Speakers of Other Languages (National Standard)* and the 1500 Commonly Used High Frequency Chinese Vocabulary, along with the Common European Framework of Reference for Languages (CEFR) to design the "Rainbow Bridge" vocabulary grading standard. The series is divided into seven levels (Starter*, Level 1, Level 2, Level 3, Level 4, Level 5 and Level 6) for students at different stages in their Chinese education to choose from. For each level, new words are no more than 20% of the vocabulary amount as specified in the corresponding HSK and CEFR levels.

---

* Represented by "S" on the back cover.

As the levels progress, the passage length will in turn increase. The following table indicates the corresponding "Rainbow Bridge" level, HSK and CEFR levels, the vocabulary amount, and number of characters.

Level	Starter	1	2	3	4	5	6
HSK/ CEFR Level	HSK1 CEFR A1	HSK1-2 CEFR A1-A2	HSK2-3 CEFR A2-B1	HSK3 CEFR A2-B1	HSK3-4 CEFR B1	HSK4 CEFR B1-B2	HSK5 CEFR B2-C1
Vocabulary	150	300	500	750	1000	1500	2500
Characters	1000	2500	5000	7500	10,000	15,000	25,000

II. Intriguing stories on various themes. The series features engaging stories known for their twists and turns as well as deeply touching plots. The readers will find it a joyful experience to read the stories. The topics are selected from Chinese mythology, legends, folklore, literary classics, biographies of renowned people and historical tales. Such widely ranged topics would exert an invisible, yet formative, influence on readers' understanding of Chinese culture and history.

III. Reasonably structured and easy to use. For each volume of the "Rainbow Bridge" series, apart from a Chinese story, we also provide an introduction to the main characters in Chinese and English, new words with English explanations and sample sentences, and an English translation of the story, followed by comprehension exercises and a vocabulary list to help users read and understand the story and improve their Chinese reading skills. The exercises are mainly presented as objective questions that take on various forms with moderate difficulty. Moreover, keys to the exercises are also provided. The series can be used by teachers in class or by students for self-study.

If you have any questions, comments or suggestions about the series, please email us at liuxiaolin@sinolingua.com.cn. You can also exchange ideas with us via our WeChat account: CHQRainbowBridge. This account will provide updates on the series along with Chinese reading materials and cultural tips.

Han Ying and Liu Xiaolin

十兄弟的奇特本领

The unique skills of the ten brothers

大　哥 (dà gē)：看得很远。
The oldest brother could see very far.

二　哥 (èr gē)：听得很远。
The second brother could detect sound from far away.

三　哥 (sān gē)：会飞。
The third brother could fly.

四　哥 (sì gē)：力气很大。
The fourth brother had herculean strength.

五　哥 (wǔ gē)：手很长。
The fifth brother could stretch his arms to an extrodinary length.

六　哥 (liù gē)：腿很长。
The sixth brother had long legs.

七　哥 (qī gē)：头砍不坏。
The seventh brother's head can't be cut off.

八　哥 (bā gē)：会喷火。
The eighth brother could spew hot flames from his mouth.

九　哥 (jiǔ gē)：眼泪能把人冲走。
The ninth brother's tears could carry one away like a raging river.

小弟弟 (xiǎo dìdi)：会吹大风。
The youngest brother could blow strong wind.

中文故事

十兄弟①

① 兄弟 (xiōngdì) n. brother
e.g., 他们两个是兄弟。

② 捡 (jiǎn) v. pick up, gather
e.g., 我在路上捡了一个钱包

③ 珠子 (zhūzi) n. pearl, bead
e.g., 这个珠子真大。

很多年前，有一对老夫妻，他们结婚很多年了，一直没有孩子。有一天，丈夫在外面捡②到了十个珠子③。珠子大大的，很漂亮，妻子也很喜欢。

一个有钱人听说了这件事,很想得到这十个珠子,就跑来对丈夫说:"听说你捡了十个珠子,能让我看看吗?"

丈夫把珠子拿出来,有钱人一看就喜欢,说:"你们没钱,要这珠子有什么用?你把它们卖给我吧。"

丈夫生气地说:"我虽然没有钱,可是也很喜欢这珠子,所以我不能卖给你。"

① 皇帝 (huángdì) n. emperor
e.g., 中国有过很多皇帝。

有钱人就跑去对皇帝①说："有人有十个漂亮的珠子，应该送给你。他如果不给你，你就叫人去要过来。"

皇帝听了，真的叫人去要珠子。妻子很生气，就把珠子都吃了下去。

① 抓 (zhuā) v. arrest, catch
e.g., 警察把小偷抓走了。

皇帝的人找不到十个珠子，就打了丈夫，还把他抓① 走了。

到了晚上，妻子的肚子①疼了起来，她生②下了十个儿子！这十兄弟很快就长大了，每个人都有自己的本领③。

① 肚子 (dùzi) n. belly, abdomen
e.g., 我的肚子很疼。

② 生 (shēng) v. give birth to
e.g., 她生了两个孩子。

③ 本领 (běnlǐng) n. skill, ability
e.g., 我爬树的本领很强。

① 保护 (bǎohù) v.
protect
e.g., 他保护了我们。

有一天，十兄弟问妈妈："妈妈，我们的爸爸在哪里？"妈妈哭着对他们说："为了保护①我们，爸爸被皇帝的人抓走了。"

他们一听爸爸被皇帝抓走了,就对妈妈说:"我们一定要找到爸爸,把他救①出来!"

① 救 (jiù) v. rescue, save
e.g., 十兄弟把他们的爸爸救出来了。

① 哥 (gē) *n.* elder brother
e.g., 他是我哥哥。

② 皇宫 (huánggōng) *n.* palace
e.g., 皇帝住在皇宫里面。

③ 卫兵 (wèibīng) *n.* guard
e.g., 这里有很多卫兵。

大哥① 看得很远，他看到爸爸被关在皇宫② 里面，外面还有很多卫兵③。

二哥听得很远,他听到卫兵们说:"如果这个人不把珠子给皇帝,我们就把他拉出去砍头①。"

① 砍头 (kǎn tóu) v. behead
e.g., 卫兵要把这个人拉出去砍头。

十兄弟知道皇帝要砍爸爸的头，都很着急，就在晚上跑到皇宫里去救爸爸。

皇宫的墙①很高。三哥会飞②，他飞进皇宫，从里面把门③打开，十兄弟就都进去了。

① 墙 (qiáng) *n.* wall
e.g., 这墙真高。

② 飞 (fēi) *v.* fly
e.g., 小鸟飞上了天。

③ 门 (mén) *n.* gate, door
e.g., 这是皇宫的大门。

① 力气 (lìqi) n. strength
e.g., 我哥哥的力气很大。

② 屋子 (wūzi) n. room
e.g., 这是我的屋子。

③ 手 (shǒu) n. hand
e.g., 我们都有两只手。

④ 推 (tuī) v. push
e.g., 我用力推开了窗户。

四哥的力气① 很大。他找到关爸爸的屋子②，用手③ 一推④，就把门推开了。门打开后，十兄弟一看，爸爸不在里面。

五哥的手很长，他用长手抓到一个卫兵，问他爸爸在哪里。卫兵说，皇帝要砍爸爸的头，已经命令①人把他拉出皇宫去了。

① 命令 (mìnglìng) v. order
e.g., 他命令我现在就去打扫房间。

① 腿 (tuǐ) *n.* leg
e.g., 人有腿才能走路。
② 背 (bēi) *v.* carry ... on the back
e.g., 我来背你。

六哥的腿①很长。他背②起七哥，一下就走到了皇宫外面，找到了爸爸。

七哥对卫兵说:"我是这个老人的儿子,你们不要砍他的头了,来砍我的头吧!"卫兵就来砍七哥的头。可是不管①卫兵怎么砍,七哥的头一点儿事都没有。

① 不管 (bùguǎn) *conj.* no matter...; despite
e.g., 不管你说什么,我都要去做这件事。

① 追 (zhuī) *v.* chase, run after
e.g., 你追不到我。

六哥看到卫兵忙着砍七哥的头，背起爸爸就跑。卫兵看到了，想要去追①。就在这时候，兄弟们都来了。

八哥对六哥说:"你们先走,看我的!"他喷①出大火②,烧③死了很多卫兵。

① 喷 (pēn) v. spurt, spew
e.g., 他喷了一口水。

② 火 (huǒ) n. fire, flame
e.g., 外面着火了。

③ 烧 (shāo) v. burn
e.g., 大火烧了三天。

① 眼泪 (yǎnlèi) n.
tear
e.g., 你怎么流眼泪了?

② 冲 (chōng) v.
wash, flush
e.g., 这里的房屋被大水冲了。

九哥说:"我来了!"他坐在地上大哭,眼泪① 把卫兵都冲② 跑了。

小弟弟对着皇宫吹①风,快要把皇宫吹倒了。皇帝着急地说:"不要吹了,不要吹了!我不要珠子了,你们可以回家了!"

① 吹 (chuī) *v.* blow
e.g., 水太热了,喝之前要先吹吹。

十兄弟高高兴兴地和爸爸回家了。妈妈看到十兄弟和爸爸都回来了，也很高兴。

有了十个能干[①]的儿子，他们过得一天比一天好，一家人在一起很快乐。

> ① 能干 (nénggàn)
> *adj.* able, capable, competent
> e.g., 这个孩子已经会做饭了，真能干！

> English Version

Ten Brothers

A long time ago, there was an old couple. They had been married for many years and still didn't have any child. One day, the husband went back home with ten pearls. The pearls were big and beautiful so his wife liked them very much.

A rich man heard about this and wanted to take the ten pearls for himself. He found the husband and said to him, "I heard you have ten pearls. May I have a look at them?"

The husband showed him the pearls. The rich man grew very fond of them at first sight and said, "You are poor. What can you make of the pearls? Sell them to me."

The husband replied angrily, "Poor as I am, I like the pearls very much. I wouldn't sell them to you."

The rich man went to see the emperor and said to him, "A man has ten beautiful pearls. He should have offered them to you. If he doesn't offer them, you should send people to get them."

The emperor listened to him and sent his guards for the pearls. The wife became angry and swallowed the pearls.

Since the emperor's guards couldn't find the ten pearls, they beat the husband and took him away.

On that evening, the wife's stomach began to ache and later she gave birth to ten sons. The ten sons grew up at an abnormal pace and each one of them had a unique skill.

One day, they asked their mother, "Mom, where is our dad?" Their mother wept, "To protect us, your dad was taken away by the emperor's guards."

Knowing their father was taken away by the emperor, the brothers said to their mother, "We must find our father and rescue him!"

The oldest brother could see very far. He saw that their father was imprisoned at the royal palace and many guards stationed outside the palace.

The second brother could detect sound from far away. He heard the guards say, "If this man still refused to offer the pearls to the emperor, he will be beheaded."

The ten brothers were extremely worried after they learned that the emperor wanted to behead their father. They ran to the palace to rescue him that very evening.

The walls of the palace were very high. The third brother could fly, so he flew over the wall and opened the gate from the inside and let his brothers in.

The fourth brother had herculean strength. When they reached the room where their dad was imprisoned, he pushed the door open easily. Looking into the open door, they found their father was not in the room.

The fifth brother could stretch his arms to an extraordinary length. He caught a guard with one arm and demanded to know where they took their father. The guard told them that their father was taken outside of the palace to be beheaded on the emperor's order.

The sixth brother had long legs. He carried the seventh brother on his back and reached the outside of the palace in one stride. They found their father there.

Seven said to the guards, "I'm his son. Don't behead him. Cut off my head instead!" The guards went to cut Seven's head off. No matter how hard they tried, Seven's head stayed well on his shoulders.

Seeing the guards were too busy trying to behead Seven, the sixth brother carried their father away. The guards noticed immediately and chased after them. At that moment, the rest of the brothers arrived.

Eight said to the sixth brother, "You go first. I'll get your back!" He spewed hot flames from his mouth, burning many guards to death.

Nine said, "I'm here!" and started to cry sitting on the ground. His tears carried the guards away like a raging river.

Ten, the youngest brother, blew the palace so hard that it was going to collapse. The emperor said anxiously, "Stop that! Stop that! I don't want the pearls anymore! You can go back home."

The ten brothers went back home happily with their father. Their mother was incredibly happy to see all of them back.

With ten capable sons, their life was getting better and better. The family lived happily together from that point onward.

课前练习 Warm-up exercises

一、朗读下面的短语。Read the following phrases.

jiùchū bàba　　bēiqǐ qī gē　　pēnchū dà huǒ
救出爸爸　　背起七哥　　喷出大火

chōngzǒu wèibīng　　chuīdǎo huánggōng
冲走卫兵　　吹倒皇宫

二、思考题。Pre-reading questions.

1. 十兄弟都有什么本领？

2. 他们是怎么救出爸爸的？

课后练习 Reading exercises

一、连线题。 Match.

请为十兄弟选择对应的本领并连线。

A. 大哥　　　　a. 会喷火

B. 二哥　　　　b. 腿很长

C. 三哥　　　　c. 会飞

D. 四哥　　　　d. 眼泪能冲走卫兵

E. 五哥　　　　e. 力气很大

F. 六哥　　　　f. 听得很远

G. 七哥　　　　g. 看得很远

H. 八哥　　　　h. 手很长

I. 九哥　　　　i. 头砍不坏

J. 小弟弟　　　j. 会吹风

二、为下列各题选择正确的答案。
Choose the correct answer according to the story.

1. 有钱人想买珠子，丈夫不卖，因为（　　　）。

　　A. 有钱人给的钱少　　　B. 他不喜欢有钱人

　　C. 他想把珠子送给皇帝　D. 他也很喜欢珠子

2. 皇帝的卫兵（　　）。

　　A. 拿走了珠子　　　　B. 抓走了十兄弟的爸爸

　　C. 吃了珠子　　　　　D. 烧死了十兄弟的爸爸

3. 皇帝要杀十兄弟的爸爸，因为（　　）。

　　A. 他没有把珠子卖给有钱人

　　B. 他有十个儿子

　　C. 他不说出十个珠子在哪里

　　D. 他拿走了皇帝的珠子

4. 以下内容跟故事不符的是（　　）。

　　A. 六哥的腿很长，他跳进皇宫，从里面打开了大门

　　B. 八哥喷出的大火烧死了很多卫兵

　　C. 九哥的眼泪冲走了卫兵

　　D. 小弟弟快要把皇宫吹倒了

5. 以下内容正确的是（　　）。

　　A. 大哥救出了爸爸

　　B. 七哥救出了爸爸

　　C. 小弟弟救出了爸爸

　　D. 十兄弟一起救出了爸爸

三、判断题：请根据故事内容判断下列说法是否正确，如果正确请标"T"，不正确请标"F"。
Decide whether the following statements are true (T) or false (F).

1. 老夫妻结婚很多年都没有孩子。　　　　　　（　）
2. 妻子很饿，把十个珠子吃了。　　　　　　　（　）
3. 妻子吃了十个珠子后，生出了十个兄弟。　　（　）
4. 大哥听到皇帝说要杀死爸爸。　　　　　　　（　）
5. 九哥没有本领，只会哭。　　　　　　　　　（　）

四、看图复述故事内容。Fill in the blanks to retell the story using the pictures.

1. 十兄弟知道皇帝要砍爸爸的头，_____，就在晚上跑到皇宫里去救爸爸。

2.五哥的手很长，_____，问他爸爸在哪里。

3.可是不管卫兵怎么砍，七哥的头_____。

4. 九哥坐在地上大哭,眼泪_____。

5. 妈妈看到_____。

课后练习答案 Keys to the exercises

一、连线题
A-g, B-f, C-c, D-e, E-h,
F-b, G-i, H-a, I-d, J-j

二、为下列各题选择正确的答案
1. D 2. B 3. C 4. A 5. D

三、判断题：请根据故事内容判断下列说法是否正确，如果正确请标"T"，不正确请标"F"
1. T 2. F 3. T 4. F 5. F

四、看图复述故事内容
1. 很着急
2. 他用长手抓到一个卫兵
3. 一点儿事都没有
4. 把卫兵都冲走了
5. 十兄弟和爸爸都回来了，很高兴

词汇表
Vocabulary List

保护	v.	bǎohù	protect
背	v.	bēi	carry … on the back
本领	n.	běnlǐng	skill, ability
不管	conj.	bùguǎn	no matter..., despite
冲	v.	chōng	wash, flush
吹	v.	chuī	blow
肚子	n.	dùzi	belly, abdomen
飞	v.	fēi	fly
哥	n.	gē	elder brother
皇帝	n.	huángdì	emperor
皇宫	n.	huánggōng	palace
火	n.	huǒ	fire, flame
捡		jiǎn	pick up, gather
救	v.	jiù	rescue, save
砍头	v.	kǎn tóu	behead
力气	n.	lìqi	strength
门	n.	mén	gate, door
命令	v.	mìnglìng	order
能干	adj.	nénggàn	able, capable, competent
喷	v.	pēn	spurt, spew
墙	n.	qiáng	wall
烧	v.	shāo	burn
生	v.	shēng	give birth to
手	n.	shǒu	hand
推	v.	tuī	push
腿	n.	tuǐ	leg
卫兵	n.	wèibīng	guard
屋子	n.	wūzi	room
兄弟	n.	xiōngdì	brother
眼泪	n.	yǎnlèi	tear
珠子	n.	zhūzi	pearl, bead
抓	v.	zhuā	arrest, catch
追	v.	zhuī	chase, run after

项目策划：韩　颖　刘小琳
责任编辑：韩　颖
英文编辑：范逊敏
英文翻译：张　乐
封面设计：E·T创意工作室

图书在版编目（CIP）数据

十兄弟：汉、英 / 叶婵娟改编. — 北京：华语教学出版社，2016
（"彩虹桥"汉语分级读物. 入门级：150词）
ISBN 978-7-5138-1064-7

Ⅰ. ①十… Ⅱ. ①叶… Ⅲ. ①汉语－对外汉语教学－语言读物 Ⅳ. ①H195.5

中国版本图书馆CIP数据核字（2015）第 263023 号

十兄弟

叶婵娟　改编

*

©华语教学出版社有限责任公司
华语教学出版社有限责任公司出版
（中国北京百万庄大街24号　邮政编码 100037）
电话：(86)10-68320585　68997826
传真：(86)10-68997826　68326333
网址：www.sinolingua.com.cn
电子信箱：hyjx@sinolingua.com.cn
新浪微博地址：http://weibo.com/sinolinguavip
北京京华虎彩印刷有限公司印刷
2016年（32开）第1版
2016年第1版第1次印刷
（汉英）
ISBN 978-7-5138-1064-7
定价：15.00元